Getting To Know...

Nature's Children

SQUIRRELS

George Peck

SCHOLASTIC INC.

New York   Toronto   London   Auckland   Sydney
Mexico City   New Delhi   Hong Kong   Buenos Aires

Facts in Brief

Classification of North American tree squirrels

Class: *Mammalia* (mammals)

Order: *Rodentia* (rodents)

Family: *Sciuridae* (shade-tailed family)

Genus: *Sciurus* (Gray Squirrel, also includes Fox Squirrel)

Tamiasciurus (Red Squirrel)

Species: Several species of both Gray and Red Squirrels

World distribution. The genus *sciurus* is widespread in Europe and Asia, and in North, Central, and South America. The genus *tamiasciurus* is found only in North America.

Habitat. Found in all wooded areas where there is sufficient food.

Habits. Active mainly during the day. Usually nests in tree holes. In summer many construct a nest, called a drey, made of twigs and leaves. Gathers large food supply in the fall.

Diet. Especially fond of nuts, but also eat buds, flowers, and berries. Will sometimes eat birds' eggs or snails. The Red Squirrel has most wide-ranging appetite.

Published by Scholastic Inc.
90 Old Sherman Turnpike, Danbury, Connecticut 06816.

SCHOLASTIC and associated logos are trademarks of Scholastic Inc.

ISBN 0-7172-6704-0   Printed in the U.S.A.

Edited by: Elizabeth Grace Zuraw   *Photo Editor:* Nancy Norton
Photo Rights: Ivy Images   *Cover Design*: Niemand Design

Have you ever wondered . . .

what squirrels are famous for? page 5

how many kinds of squirrels there are? page 9

why many Gray Squirrels like to live in cities? page 10

where Red Squirrels like to live? page 10

how big a squirrel's home range may be? page 13

what squirrels do when they are annoyed? page 14

if all Gray Squirrels are gray? page 17

which is bigger, a Red Squirrel or a Gray Squirrel? page 17

how squirrels run on icy branches without slipping? page 18

what squirrels use their tails for? page 21

how a squirrel in a hurry gets down from a tree? page 21

if squirrels have good eyesight? page 22

what squirrels come down to the ground for? page 22

if a squirrel has many enemies? page 25

what squirrel homes are like? page 26

if squirrels are good housekeepers? page 29

how squirrels spend their days? page 30

what squirrels like to eat? page 33

how squirrels crack nuts? page 34

how squirrels get ready for winter? page 37

what newborn squirrels look like? page 41

if a mother squirrel takes good care of her young? page 42

how fast baby squirrels grow? page 45

when young squirrels are ready to go out on their own? page 46

Words To Know page 47

Index page 48

If you like to keep a good supply of something stashed away, you've probably been told that you're behaving like a squirrel—you're "squirreling away" that item. Squirrels are famous for their habit of gathering and storing nuts. But besides collecting and storing, squirrels are also known for chattering and scolding and performing amazing treetop acrobatics. They love chasing each other up and down trees and leaping from one tree to another, chattering noisily when they stop for a break. And if you've ever seen a dog go after a squirrel, you know just how noisy a squirrel can get.

No matter where you live—in a town or in the country—you probably have squirrel neighbors nearby. Many things that squirrels do will be familiar to you. But have you ever wondered where baby squirrels are born? Or where squirrels spend the winter? Or how squirrels can walk along wires or straight down brick walls, without falling?

Read on to find out the answers to these and many other squirrel questions.

Almost Ready—But Not Quite

By the age of three months, young squirrels are scampering through the treetops and fending for themselves. Before that, their home in a tree is snug and safe, while the outside world probably looks pretty big and scary.

Adult tree squirrels are bold and curious, but very young squirrels are quite timid. They're likely to run for cover at the slightest hint of anything strange or dangerous. These young ones probably haven't yet gone very far from the nest, but they're getting bigger and braver every day. Soon their curiosity will overcome their nervousness and they'll be ready to face the world on their own.

It doesn't take a young squirrel long to master the acrobatic skills that this animal is noted for.

Meet the Relatives

The squirrel family is a large one. There are about 50 different kinds of squirrels. And squirrels of one kind or another are found almost everywhere in the world. The only places without squirrels are the desert areas of Egypt and Arabia and the southern parts of the world such as Australia, New Zealand, and the tip of South America.

In North America, there are squirrels that live mainly in trees and squirrels that live in *burrows,* holes dug in the ground. The burrow-living squirrels include Prairie Dogs, marmots, woodchucks, chipmunks, and Ground Squirrels. The tree squirrels include the Gray Squirrel, Fox Squirrel, Flying Squirrel, and Red Squirrel. The tree squirrels that most North Americans know best are the Gray Squirrel and the Red Squirrel.

Squirrels spend much of their time searching for food—and stopping for an occasional snack.

Where Gray Squirrels live in North America

Opposite page: *Winter won't bother this chubby fur ball. Not only do squirrels grow an extra thick coat in the fall, they also eat a lot of food to store fat for the cold months ahead.*

Squirrels Everywhere

Gray Squirrels are found mainly in southern Canada and the eastern United States. Many Gray Squirrels are city dwellers. One reason is that cities are safe places to live: few squirrel enemies live there.

Cities are also good places for squirrels to find handouts. Many people supply squirrels with tidbits to eat, sometimes on purpose, but other times not. Almost anyone who puts out seed for the birds has watched squirrels move in and gobble the seed up. To discourage these food snatchers, many bird feeders are equipped with metal collars designed to keep squirrels from climbing up. Even so, bird feeders are still a good source of food for squirrels. Birds scatter seed on the ground as they feed, and squirrels are quick to clean up after them.

Red Squirrels are found all across Canada and in several parts of the United States. They live almost anywhere there are forests. But unlike Gray Squirrels, they're seldom seen in towns and cities. They're not very neighborly and prefer to live alone in the wild.

Squirrel Territory

Gray Squirrels spend most of their time in their home *range* or *territory,* the area in which they live. The female's range may be about 5 to 15 acres (2 to 6 hectares). The male's is larger, sometimes as big as 50 acres (20 hectares). Gray Squirrels are quite happy to share their home range with other squirrels and birds.

Where Red Squirrels live in North America

Red Squirrels, on the other hand, are much more exclusive. Once a Red Squirrel has claimed a territory as its home base, it'll usually chase or frighten away anything that it considers a trespasser. Trespassers might include crows and jays, as well as other squirrels. A Red Squirrel's territory is usually about 2 acres (close to 1 hectare), but it might be larger or smaller depending on how much food is available.

Red Squirrels are especially active just after sunrise and just before sunset.

Squirrel Chatter

Next time you take a quiet walk in the woods, listen for the sound of squirrels "talking."

If a Red Squirrel is puzzled, it sometimes makes a soft *whuck whuck* sound. But you're more likely to hear a loud, rough *tcherr tcherr*.

This is a Red Squirrel's scolding call. If you can see the squirrel, you'll probably find that it's stamping its feet and jerking its tail as it calls. The message is clear: "Get out of my territory!"

A Gray Squirrel makes similar calls when it's threatened or annoyed. It also flicks its tail to signal its moods. A Gray Squirrel threatens intruders by fluffing its tail and jerking it rapidly. When the squirrel is only mildly upset, it just waves its tail rapidly. A gentle flick of the tail is a sign of greeting.

Half of the length of the Gray Squirrel's body is its tail. The tail is often used for communicating many different moods.

Squirrels Up Close

Red Squirrels have a reddish-brown coat, a white underside, and a white ring around the eyes. In the summer, a black stripe on both sides of the squirrel's body separates the red coat from the white underside. In winter, the Red Squirrel's coat is darker and thicker, with no side stripe. Instead, a single orange-red stripe runs down the *middle* of its back.

Size Comparison

Gray Squirrel

Not all Gray Squirrels are gray. Some are black or even a reddish color. Since Gray Squirrels are quite a bit bigger than Red Squirrels, it's unlikely that you'd mistake a reddish Gray Squirrel for a Red Squirrel.

Red Squirrel

An adult Gray Squirrel is usually about 20 inches (50 centimeters) long from the tip of its nose to the end of its bushy tail. Red Squirrels are generally a little more than half that length when fully grown.

The black stripe on the side of this Red Squirrel's body shows that the squirrel is wearing its summer coat.

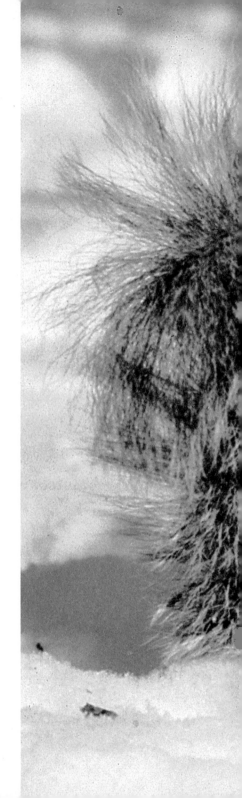

Summer and Winter Coats

Do you have different jackets for winter and summer? If so, you have something in common with squirrels. In the summer, squirrels have a lightweight coat to keep cool. They get the light coat by *molting,* or shedding their winter fur. Then in the fall, they grow a thicker coat of fur, to keep them warm in the winter.

A squirrel's winter coat is actually two coats in one. A thin layer of short fur, called *underfur,* traps body-warmed air next to the body. Longer *guard hairs,* which make up the outer layer of the coat, shed water and snow. In winter, even the soles of a squirrel's feet grow fur. This helps keep the squirrel warm and also gives the animal a better grip on wet or icy branches.

A thick fur coat keeps a Gray Squirrel cozy all winter. Its bushy tail serves as a blanket, too, when the animal curls up.

18

Treetop Acrobats

Circus acrobats must envy squirrels. These furry athletes are as much at home in the trees as we humans are on the ground. They use their strong, sharp claws to dig into a tree's rough bark. This makes them so surefooted, they can climb down trees headfirst, and even climb up brick walls! And squirrels can travel quite far without ever touching the ground— they just jump from tree to tree. As they leap from branch to branch, their tails act as rudders that help them keep their balance.

If squirrels want to get to the ground quickly, they simply jump. By spreading their legs and holding their tails out, they can glide just enough to break their fall. Red Squirrels have jumped or fallen from branches as high as 118 feet (36 meters) above the ground without being hurt. Jumps of about 30 feet (9 meters) are normal.

A flying squirrel doesn't actually fly. It glides through the air, using the wide flaps of skin along its sides to slow its movement.

Life on the Ground

Sharp claws for grabbing and a rudder-like tail for steering are not the squirrel's only acrobatic equipment. The squirrel also has excellent eyesight, which helps it know exactly how far to leap to get to the next branch safely.

Even though squirrels spend much of their time in the trees, they often come down to the ground to look for food and to store it, or to get to another tree that's too far away to reach by jumping. Squirrels usually walk slowly when feeding on the ground, but if danger threatens, they can bound over to the nearest tree and scoot up it in no time. A squirrel can cover about 6 feet (2 meters) in one bound and can run about 15 miles (24 kilometers) per hour over a short distance.

In some parts of the country, Gray Squirrels have dark or black fur. Tree squirrels such as the Gray Squirrel have ancestors going as far back as 28 million years.

Watch Out!

Squirrels have to be on the alert constantly because there are many animals, called *predators,* that view them as a tasty meal. Squirrels must be particularly on the lookout for predators such as coyotes, foxes, skunks, raccoons, wolves, lynx, bobcats, and some kinds of hawks and owls. But a squirrel's most dangerous enemies are some kinds of weasels—agile animals that climb trees and are almost as surefooted as squirrels.

To escape from weasels and other tree-climbing enemies, squirrels must move very fast or find a small space to duck into. Most squirrels soon get to know every nook and cranny in their range. They know where all the best hiding places are, and are lightning-quick in taking cover in one of them when chased.

A squirrel is usually quite safe in its tree hideaway—where it would quickly scamper if it were to spot an enemy.

A squirrel's drey

Opposite page:
A home in the hollow of a tree is more than safe— it's also a cozy place in winter for this Red Squirrel.

Tree Houses

Many squirrels make their home high up in trees. In winter—and in spring and summer when they're raising a family—they usually make a *den,* or animal home, in a hole in a tree. It could be a natural hole or a deserted woodpecker home. If no holes are available, squirrels often build large nests of twigs and leaves. These nests are called *dreys.*

If you saw a drey, you might mistake it for a shaggy pile of leaves and twigs that got caught in the fork of a tree. Actually, a drey is a carefully woven, waterproof house with a small entranceway that leads into a round snug room lined with pine needles.

Some Red Squirrels spend winters in ground dens they make in fallen trees or rockpiles or under tree roots. In summer, they build nests in trees or take over old crow or hawk nests.

Red Squirrels usually live alone, but they sometimes share a nest or den with their young for a winter. Gray Squirrels are much more sociable. Sometimes as many as six Grays will cuddle up together in a drey.

Clean—But Messy

Squirrels are very careful to keep their coats clean. They spend a lot of time *grooming,* or licking and cleaning their fur and combing it with their paws. Grooming is important because clean and fluffy hair insulates the squirrel from both hot and cold. A well-groomed fur coat traps a layer of air against the squirrel's skin.

A squirrel's tail, if kept clean and bushy, is useful in several ways. The tail curls easily over the squirrel's back and head. On a hot summer day, the turned-up tail puts the squirrel in the cool shadow of its tail. In fact, the word *squirrel* comes from two Greek words that mean "shadow tail." And in the rain, the squirrel can throw up its tail and use it as an umbrella!

But even though squirrels keep themselves very clean, they're not very good housekeepers. When their nests or dens get littered with twigs, leaves, and dirt, they simply move instead of cleaning up. Imagine what would happen if your family never bothered to take out its trash! You'd probably have to move often, too.

Opposite page: *A squirrel's tongue may be little but it does a big job in grooming this animal's fur coat.*

Fair-weather Days

In spring, summer, and fall, a squirrel's day starts at sunrise. Depending on what needs to be done, the squirrel spends the first few hours of the day bustling about, either getting itself a meal, gathering and storing food, or gathering nesting materials.

By midday, the squirrel is ready for a rest. And what better way to relax than to bask in the sun or curl up in a cozy nest for an afternoon nap? Toward the end of the day, the squirrel may go out again in search of food. A squirrel spends a lot of time looking for food. It eats up to 2 pounds (nearly 1 kilogram) of food a week.

Both Gray Squirrels and Red Squirrels are most active during the day, but they're occasionally seen out looking for a snack on a moonlit summer night.

Squirrels need liquid every day. They get most of it from eating fruits and berries, but sometimes they dip into a stream for a drink of water. In winter you might see a squirrel eat snow.

Red Squirrels will gnaw on old bones and antlers they find on the forest floor. They're also fond of mushrooms and can safely eat even those that are deadly to people!

A Varied Menu

Did you know that squirrels help plant our forests? They collect nuts and store them in shallow holes that they dig in the ground. Later, the squirrels dig up and eat some of the nuts, but they bury so many nuts that they never find them all. The lost nuts often take root and, in time, grow into new trees.

While squirrels have a definite preference for nuts, they also eat many other kinds of food, including buds, flowers, seeds, berries, fruit, and mushrooms. Most squirrels will also eat insects, grubs, and birds' eggs if they come across them.

Red Squirrels are a bit more enthusiastic about meat than other squirrels. They dine occasionally on snails, small birds, mice, and even young rabbits. The Red Squirrel's wide-ranging appetite helps to explain why it's found in so many different *habitats,* or kinds of places animals naturally live in. The Red Squirrel can get itself a meal just about anywhere.

A Built-in Nutcracker

Opposite page:
When there's snow on the ground, squirrels rely on their keen sense of smell to find nuts they've buried. They don't locate them from memory. Sometimes squirrels have to dig through several feet of snow to get to the buried food.

Squirrels are *rodents*—animals that have a certain kind of teeth that are especially good for gnawing. A squirrel has two pairs of large, sharp front teeth called *incisors*. These teeth wear down, but they never stop growing. They're sharpened by rubbing against each other as the squirrel uses them. A squirrel's incisors may grow about 6 inches (about 15 centimeters) a year, but are worn down by use.

With these powerful teeth, a squirrel can quickly and easily crack open the hardest nut to get at the tasty meat or kernel inside. The squirrel holds the nut between its nimble front paws, often turning the nut around while removing the tough outer husk.

Next time you pass under an oak or walnut tree in the fall, look carefully at the ground around it. You might spot bits of shells and husks. That'll tell you that a squirrel has recently been feasting in the branches above you. But watch out! One may still be up there, dropping nuts on unsuspecting people passing by below.

Brrr! It's Cold Outside!

Tree squirrels, unlike some of their burrow-dwelling cousins, do not *hibernate,* or go into a long sleep during the winter. Instead, they remain active, staying in their dens only during severe storms and blizzards. In Alaska, Red Squirrels have been seen outside on days when the temperature has fallen as low as -29 degrees Fahrenheit (-34 degrees Celsius).

Food is scarce in winter, so squirrels gather and store it in the fall. They do this by *instinct*— a strong inborn pattern of behavior that animals are born with. Instinct enables squirrels to gather and store food without thinking about it.

Squirrels store food in different ways, depending on the food. Hard nuts are stored singly in shallow holes the squirrels dig in the ground. A squirrel can bury one nut a minute! The cones of evergreen trees are piled into a hollow tree stump or next to a rock or log and then covered with leaves. One pile may contain hundreds of cones. Soft foods such as fruit or mushrooms are laid in the forks of trees to dry out, and then are stored.

Opposite page: *The fox squirrel measures up to 29 inches (74 centimeters). It's the largest squirrel in the United States. Its tail makes up half of its length.*

Starting a Family

Gray Squirrels *mate,* or come together to produce young, in January. Red Squirrels mate in February and March. Both kinds of squirrels sometimes mate again in the summer. Mating season is a busy time. A number of male squirrels will chase a female who has signaled that she is ready to mate. These chases often last for quite a long time and are accompanied by much chattering and tail twitching. There seldom are fights among the males, but there is a lot of scolding and some pushing, until the female chooses one of the males as her mate.

Usually the male leaves the female after mating, but sometimes the pair stays together to build a nest. But the male is always gone by the time the babies arrive.

Squirrels are ready to start having families when they're a year old. Vying for a female's attention, males often angrily scold each other.

Tiny Babies

After mating, the female starts preparing a home for her babies. She prefers the comfort and safety of a tree den, but if no tree holes are available, she'll build a drey. In either case, she pays particular attention to furnishing her nursery. It will be well lined with strips of bark and leaves to make a soft, warm place for the babies.

Opposite page: *Newborn Red Squirrels must wait almost a month before their eyes open.*

About a month and a half after mating, the mother squirrel gives birth to a litter of babies. *Litter* is the name for the group of young animals that are born together. A Red Squirrel mother usually has a litter of three to five young, although she may have fewer than that or as many as eight. Gray Squirrel families are usually slightly smaller.

Baby squirrels are born tiny, pink, and naked. Their eyes and ears are sealed shut, and they have no teeth. Red Squirrel newborns are about 3 inches (8 centimeters) long and weigh less than a quarter of an ounce (7 grams). Newborn Gray Squirrels are about twice that size.

A Devoted Mother

The mother squirrel spends a great deal of time with her babies in the first weeks of their lives. This is a private time for the mother squirrel and her family. She chases away all intruders from her den or nest as well as the area around it. Even the father squirrel isn't allowed in.

If the privacy of her den or nest is seriously threatened, a mother squirrel will sometimes move her young to a new home. To do this, she carries them one by one in her mouth, as a mother cat carries her kittens. While a mother squirrel is carrying a baby, if she meets an animal that she views as a threat, she'll set the baby down for a moment and bravely drive off the intruder.

Baby squirrels grow fast. At the age of one month, these little Grays began leaving their nest and climbing on the tree around it.

Fast-growing Babies

By the time they're three weeks old, baby squirrels have their two bottom front teeth and some hair on their backs. Their ears open by four weeks of age. Red Squirrels open their eyes by the time they're four weeks old, but Gray Squirrels may take as long as five weeks. At first the babies' eyes are a cloudy blue color, but they gradually clear until they're bright and black and the young squirrels can see properly.

During these first weeks, baby squirrels *nurse,* or drink milk from their mother's body. The rich milk helps the babies grow quickly. By seven weeks, the young squirrels start to eat some solid food. And by the time they're 10 to 12 weeks old, the babies stop nursing altogether. Instead, they now can eat the same kinds of food their mother eats.

Squirrels are well equipped to be expert climbers. Even as babies, they have sharp, curved claws—four on their front feet and five on their hind feet.

Making It on Their Own

Young squirrels are ready to look after themselves by the time they stop nursing. They'll now leave their cozy den and begin a full, active life in the trees. In the late summer, many young squirrels start building their own leaf nests in the forks of trees. At first their shelters are small and loosely made, but gradually the squirrels learn how to build better ones.

In the fall, the young squirrels, just like their parents, start preparing for winter. They collect and store a supply of food, and they may look for a good spot for a winter den. Not all young squirrels leave their mother before their first winter. Some will stay with her and share her winter home.

When spring comes again, the young squirrels are ready to start their own families in their own homes. Most squirrels live to be about five years of age, but some live three times that long and have many families over the years.

Words To Know

Burrow   A hole dug in the ground by an animal for use as a home.

Den   An animal home.

Drey   A leaf nest built by a squirrel.

Groom   To brush or clean hair or fur.

Guard hairs   Long coarse hairs that make up the outer layer of a squirrel's coat.

Habitat   The kind of place in which an animal or plant naturally lives.

Hibernate   To go into a kind of heavy sleep during the winter. When animals hibernate, their breathing and heart rate slow down, and their body temperature drops.

Incisors   Front teeth used for cutting or gnawing.

Instinct   A strong, inborn pattern of behavior.

Litter   The group of young animals born together.

Mate   To come together to produce young. Either member of an animal pair is also the other's mate.

Molting   The process of shedding a coat of fur and growing another.

Nurse   To drink milk from the mother's body.

Predator   An animal that hunts other animals for food.

Range   The area that an animal lives in.

Rodent   An animal with a certain kind of teeth that are especially good for gnawing.

Territory   The area that an animal or group of animals lives in and defends from other animals of the same kind.

Underfur   Thick, short hair that traps body-warmed air next to a squirrel's body.

Index

babies, 6, 41, 42, 45, 46

chattering, 5, 14
chipmunks, 9
claws, 21, 22
climbing, 21
coats, 17, 18, 45
color, 17
communication, 14
curiosity, 6

diet, 10, 33
distribution, 9, 10
drey, 26, 29, 41

ears, 41, 45
eating, 10, 30, 45
enemies, 14, 25, 42
eyesight, 22, 41, 45

fall, 30, 34, 37, 46
feet, 18, 29, 34
female, 13, 38, 41, 42, 45
fighting, 38
flying squirrels, 9, 20
food gathering, 30, 33, 37, 46
food storing, 5, 30, 33, 37, 46

getting along, 26
Ground Squirrels, 9
grooming, 29
growing up, 45, 46

habitat, 9, 10
hibernation, 37
homes, 26, 41

jumping, 21

keeping warm, 18, 29

legs, 21
life span, 46
litter, 41

male, 13, 38, 42
marmots, 9
mating, 38
movement, 18, 21, 22,

nest, 26, 29, 38, 41, 42, 46

playing, 5
Prairie Dogs, 9

rodents, 34

size, 17, 41
sleeping, 30
spring, 30, 46
summer, 17, 18, 26, 30, 38, 46

tail, 14, 21, 38
teeth, 34, 41, 45
territory, 13, 14, 25

winter, 17, 18, 26, 37, 46
woodchucks, 9

PHOTO CREDITS

Cover: Bill Ivy. **Interiors:** *Valan Photos:* Wayne Lankinen, 4, 40; Stephen J. Krasemann,16. */Visuals Unlimited:* Gary W. Carter, 7; John C. Muegge, 15, 31; S. Maslowski, 36. /Bill Ivy, 8, 11, 12, 18-19, 23, 24, 28, 35, 43, 44. /Wayne Lankinen, 20. */Ivy Images:* Robert McCaw, 27, 32. */Thomas Stack & Associates:* Thomas Kitchin, 39.

Getting To Know...

Nature's Children

FROGS

Bill Ivy

SCHOLASTIC INC.

New York   Toronto   London   Auckland   Sydney
Mexico City   New Delhi   Hong Kong   Buenos Aires

Facts in Brief

Classification of North American frogs

Class: *Amphibia* (animals that live both on land and in the water)

Order: *Anura* (amphibians with no tails)

Family: 6 families in North America. Most common: *Ranidae* (true frogs) and *Hylidae* (tree frogs)

Species: 21 species of true frogs; 26 species of tree frogs

World distribution. Depends on species. Sixteen families worldwide with more than 2,600 species.

Habitat. All frogs are born in water and remain there as tadpoles. Most frogs move to land upon reaching adulthood, but nevertheless remain close to water.

Distinctive physical characteristics. Long sturdy hind limbs for jumping; moist smooth skin; bulging eyes; vocal sac that puffs up.

Habits. Vary with species.

Diet. Tadpoles feed on small waterplants and algae. Adult frogs eat insects, snails, slugs, worms, and small fish.

Published by Scholastic Inc.
90 Old Sherman Turnpike, Danbury, Connecticut 06816.

SCHOLASTIC and associated logos are trademarks of Scholastic Inc.

ISBN 0-7172-6704-0

Printed in the U.S.A.

Edited by: Elizabeth Grace Zuraw
Photo Rights: Ivy Images

Photo Editor: Nancy Norton
Cover Design: Niemand Design

Have you ever wondered . . .

where all frogs start their life?   page 8

how a frog's skin is different from yours?   page 11

how far a frog can jump?   page 12

if a frog can turn its head?   page 15

how a frog closes its huge eyes?   page 15

what a frog eats?   page 16

if a frog chews its food?   page 16

what a frog uses its tongue for?   page 19

why a frog always sits facing water?   page 20

why frogs sometimes puff themselves up?   page 23

how tree frogs are different from other frogs?   page 24

how a male frog attracts a mate?   page 27

how a frog can sing with its mouth closed?   page 28

how many eggs a female frog may lay?   page 31

if frog eggs have shells?   page 31

what a newly hatched tadpole looks like?   page 32

if tadpoles have many enemies?   page 35

how a tadpole changes as it becomes a frog?   page 39

what happens to the tadpole's tail?   page 40

how long the development takes from egg to frog?   page 40

what lessons a new frog has to learn?   page 43

where a frog spends the hot summer days?   page 43

what frogs do in winter?   page 44

why gardeners like to have frogs around?   page 46

Words To Know   page 47

Index   page 48

You probably know the popular fairy tale about the handsome prince who's been turned into a frog, and only a kiss can change him back into a prince again. In real life, few people would be willing to kiss a frog—unless they were sure they'd get a prince out of it! Maybe that's because many people still believe that touching a frog gives a person warts. But that's simply not true. You can't get warts from a frog—or from a toad, a close relative of the frog.

Sitting hunched on a lily pad with its bulging eyes and wide mouth, a frog appears lost in thought. And there's a lot a frog could think about. Its life is one of the most interesting in all of nature. A frog starts out as an egg that hatches into a *tadpole,* a frog hatchling that lives in water. But then it changes into a completely different creature that can walk on land! Both above and below the water, its days are full of adventure and danger.

Let's look at the different stages of a frog's life and see if Kermit, the famous Muppet, is right when he says, "It's not easy being green!"

Opposite page:
The Bullfrog is one of the largest frogs in the United States.

Overleaf:
A Leopard Frog searches moist grassy meadows for food.

Where They Live

Opposite page:
The Green Tree Frog makes its home in the southern United States.

Like toads and salamanders, the frog is an *amphibian* (am-FIB-ee-un), a Greek word meaning "two lives." Indeed, the frog does live two lives—one as a water animal and the other as a land animal.

Frogs first appeared on Earth about 180 million years ago. Today there are more than 2,600 different kinds of frogs in the world. Of these, about 35 kinds live in North America. Frogs of one type or another can be found in every U. S. state and in most of Canada. There's a kind of frog for almost every kind of *habitat,* or type of place an animal lives in. Some, such as Bullfrogs, live in big lakes. Others prefer marshes or meadows. Still others, the tree frogs, live in trees. But no matter where they live as adults, all frogs start their life in water.

Toads sometimes are mistaken for frogs, even though they aren't the same. Toads spend most of their lives on land. Frogs spend more time in the water. Frogs have fairly smooth skin; toad skin is warty. And toads, chubby and short legged, hop rather than leap. Frogs are great leapers.

Survival Skin

If you've ever held a frog, you probably
noticed how cold and clammy it feels. A
frog's skin is very different from yours. For
one thing, a frog is able to "breathe" through
its skin. That's right, a frog gets some of the
oxygen its body needs—sometimes, *all* of it—
through its skin. *Oxygen* is the part of the air
that most living things need in order to survive.
Because a frog breathes through its skin, a
frog's *blood vessels*—the tubes, arteries, and
veins through which blood flows—must be
near the surface of its body. The frog can't
afford to have layers of dry skin. Instead, it
has a moist, thin skin so that oxygen can pass
through it to the frog's blood vessels.

As the frog grows, its skin becomes tighter
and tighter. In time, the frog literally grows too
big for its skin! When the skin can stretch no
more, it splits apart into patches that gradually
fall off. Fortunately for the frog, a new layer
of skin has grown in under the old. Not one to
waste food, the newly dressed frog eats its old
coat for dinner!

Opposite page:
*With many frogs,
it's easy to tell a
male from a
female. A male's
eardrums—the
large, round disks
on each side of
the head—are
larger than his
eyes. A female's
eardrums are
usually smaller
than her eyes.*

Leapfrog, Anyone?

A frog's body is ideal for life both in and out of the water. Thanks to its powerful back legs, the frog is an excellent jumper and swimmer. Frogs seldom walk. They prefer to hop. Some species can leap an amazing 20 times their own body length. That would be the same as your long-jumping a football field!

Frogs are equally at home in the water. Each of a frog's back feet has five toes with a thin web of skin between them. Using their feet as paddles to kick, these champion swimmers glide effortlessly through the water. In fact, the design of the frog's foot is so perfect that deep diving flippers are patterned after it. Now you know why scuba divers are called frogmen!

There's no mystery in this frog's name: The Red-legged Frog has red on the undersides of its hind legs. It lives in the western United States.

A Frog's Eye View

A frog's large bulging eyes can give it a comical look. But to a frog, those silly-looking eyes have many advantages.

Opposite page: *Like all frogs, when this Bullfrog closes its eyes, they'll drop into its head.*

For you to see properly, both of your eyes must focus together on the same object. Believe it or not, at any one time, a frog's bulging eyes can look in opposite directions! This means that even though it can't turn its head, a frog can see around itself in almost a complete circle. That's why it's so hard to catch a frog by surprise.

Unlike you, a frog doesn't close its eyes by moving its eyelids. It moves its *eyes!* It pulls them deeper into their sockets, which causes the eyelids to close. And on each eye, a frog also has an extra eyelid that's transparent and blinks up from the bottom to keep the eye clean and moist. Underwater, these clear eyelids act as windows, protecting the eyes and serving as the frog's diving mask.

A frog's eyes even act as a periscope. They can poke up above the water while the rest of the frog's body stays under the surface.

Gulp!

A frog's menu is simple—if something moves, it's OK to eat! Anything small enough to fit into a frog's mouth may be sampled. Crayfish, snails, slugs, worms, fish, and insects of all kinds are potential meals if they come too close to a hungry frog.

Frogs have terrible table manners. They don't chew their food politely. Instead, a frog swallows food whole in one great big gulp. The frog stuffs larger *prey*—animals hunted for food—into its mouth using both front feet. Then the tiny teeth on the frog's upper jaw stop the meal from escaping. Incredibly, to help get its food down, the frog even blinks its eyes to pull the eyes way deep into their sockets. That helps shove the food down its throat!

A juicy worm for lunch will put a smile on any Bullfrog's face!

Sharp Shooter!

When catching small insects, the frog shows a little more class. Sitting very still, it patiently waits for dinner to arrive. When an insect comes within range, the frog attacks. Shooting out its long sticky tongue, the frog strikes the startled creature. Immediately, the frog flips its tongue back into its mouth with the tasty tidbit stuck to its tip. A frog's tongue is attached to the front of its mouth, so the frog can flip the tongue out nearly all the way. All this happens so fast that you can hardly see it. The frog is an excellent marksman and doesn't miss its target very often. It can even pick a fly right out of the air!

Opposite page: *Spring Peepers are so small, they're more often heard than seen. In spring, you can catch their loud chorus of chirping coming from the swamps and wood-lands. The chorus sounds like the distant ringing of sleigh bells.*

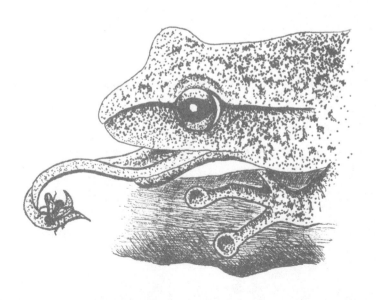

Great Escapes

A frog's life isn't all fun and games and snacking on insects. The frog has to avoid being eaten, too. It's always on the alert for *predators*—animals that hunt other animals for food. The frog's enemies include herons, otters, weasels, owls, skunks, foxes, and fish. But its most deadly enemy is the Garter Snake. A Garter Snake will gladly dine on frog at any meal.

To protect itself, the frog relies on its keen eyesight and sharp hearing. When on shore, the frog always sits facing the water. On each side of its head are two large, round eardrums that are very sensitive to sound. At the slightest crack of a twig or at the first sign of danger, the frog dives into a pond and swims to the bottom. In the water, a frog's slippery skin makes this creature as tricky to grab as a bar of soap in a tub.

When captured, the Mink Frog gives off a scent that resembles the smell of a mink or rotten onions! No wonder the odor can confuse—and quickly turn away—a predator.

Still, many frogs are caught by predators. Some frogs scream for their lives when captured. Often this sudden noise startles an enemy long enough for the frog to escape. Other frogs swallow air and puff themselves up, hoping to convince their attackers that they're much too big to swallow.

In addition, frogs rely on *camouflage,* or the color and markings on an animal that blend in with its surroundings. Some frogs, such as tree frogs, can even change color to suit their changing surroundings. Camouflage helps frogs avoid the many hungry eyes of predators that are constantly on the lookout for a meal.

Camouflage helps this Eastern Gray Tree Frog easily blend in with its surroundings.

Tree frog feet

Front

Hind

Look Up!

If you've ever gone hunting for frogs, you've probably searched along the water's edge and among tall grasses. But next time, try looking *up*. You just might see a tree frog.

Most frogs live on the ground. But tree frogs leave the water to climb up trees and shrubs after egg-laying. Using tiny suction-like disks on the tips of their toes, these expert gymnasts can scale almost any surface.

Most of the 13 kinds of tree frogs found in North America are shorter than a stick of gum and light enough to stand on a leaf. They're all great musicians and love to sing just before a thunderstorm. Their color can vary from hour to hour depending on the temperature and light. That makes them hard to see. If you hear a high trill on a hot summer's night, it could be one of these tiny songsters announcing its presence. Remember, look up!

Hanging on to leaves, bark, and even glass is easy for a tree frog—thanks to its suction-cup toes.

Musicians at the Pond

In spring, most frogs gather in ponds or marshes to *mate,* or come together to produce young, and to lay their eggs. Some types of frogs head for water in early spring, when there's still ice on it. Others, such as the Bullfrog, wait for the warmer weather—and warmer water—that come later in the spring.

When they get to their pond or marsh, the males begin to sing loudly. Sometimes, they're announcing their *territory,* the area that an animal lives in and defends. But more often, the males sing to impress the females. Each kind of frog has its own distinct call. One sounds like a man snoring. Another grunts like a pig. Still others whistle or chirp or trill like birds.

The call that people find most welcome is the Spring Peeper's high *preep-preep-preep,* the first song we hear after the long winter. But the most familiar frog voice of all belongs to the deep-voiced Bullfrog. Its loud *jug-o-rum* call echoes like a foghorn and can be heard more than half a mile (a kilometer) away! It's this call, not its size, that gives the Bullfrog its name.

Opposite page:
The Barking Tree Frog got its name from the sound it makes: a call like the bark of a dog. There are as many different frog sounds as there are kinds of frogs.

Singing with Its Mouth Closed

Have you ever wondered how a frog makes its croaks, preeps, or chirps? Believe it or not, a frog actually sings with its mouth and nostrils closed! After taking a deep breath, the frog pumps the air back and forth through its voice box into a *sac,* or pouch, in its throat or on the sides of its head. In some kinds of frogs, this vocal sac inflates to an enormous size—almost as big as the frog itself! To watch a frog sing, you might think it's actually blowing bubble gum balloons.

Surprisingly, most female frogs have very weak voices or none at all. They're simply the audience to whom all the calls are directed. But even though these females don't sing, they know the songs very well. They react only to the mating call of males of their own *species,* or kind of animals with certain traits in common.

The Western Chorus Frog, which makes its home in clearings and open fields, has a colorful vocal sac.

Eggs Galore

In the spring or early summer, the female frog deposits her eggs in the water, and the male covers them with *sperm,* a substance the male produces to start the eggs' development into tadpoles. Depending on the species of frog, a female lays anywhere from 100 to 20,000 eggs.

Unlike bird eggs, frog eggs don't have hard shells. Instead, each egg is protected by a thick layer of clear jelly that swells up in the water. The jelly also holds the eggs together. This slippery mass of tiny dark eggs is known as *spawn.* If you were to try and scoop some slippery spawn out of the water, it would simply slide right through your fingers.

The tiny tadpoles growing inside the eggs get their nourishment from their jelly covering. The tadpoles of some species of frogs are ready to hatch in a few days; others take a week or more.

Opposite page: *A female Wood Frog lays up to 1,000 or more eggs at one time. Like most frog eggs, they're dark in color.*

Hatch Day

Escaping from the jelly-like mass could be a problem for the tadpole. But luckily, by the time the tadpole has developed, the spawn has thinned out. Wriggling its little tail, the tiny tadpole swims free and attaches itself to a plant, using a sucker located under its head.

What a strange creature this newborn is! It isn't completely developed yet, so its head and body are all one, and it has no eyes or mouth. Feather-like *gills,* or openings—one on each side of its head—enable it to breathe underwater.

But, soon, eyes develop. Then its outside gills disappear and are replaced by new gills under the skin. A small, round mouth also forms, equipped with a parrot-like beak and sharp teeth. This is the perfect tool for eating tiny water plants and animals.

The tadpole has a huge appetite and almost doubles in size within a few days. At the same time, the tadpole produces a slimy film all over its body. This slippery covering helps the tadpole move more easily through the water. It also helps protect it from disease.

Peculiar Predators

Life is hazardous for the little tadpole. It has many enemies. Fish, turtles, water bugs, and birds all enjoy a tasty tadpole meal. Sometimes a Wolf Spider, while running across the water, will seize an unsuspecting tadpole and drag it to shore to be eaten later. But the strangest enemy of all is the bladderwort—a plant that actually eats tadpoles.

This bizarre plant floats in the water and has small sacs on its leaves. Each of these sacs has bristles along its edge and a trapdoor that opens from the bottom. If a careless tadpole swims too close and rubs against the plant's hairs, the trapdoor quickly opens, sucks in the surprised victim, and slams shut. Poor tadpole! There's no hope for escape once the tadpole is in the clutches of the bladderwort.

A Green Frog tadpole, like all tadpoles, is sometimes called a polliwog, *a name that comes from two old English words meaning "wiggling head."*

Frogs Forever

Opposite page:
Sitting quietly and blending in with some swamp grasses, this tadpole may be lucky enough to avoid becoming some predator's lunch. If the tadpole survives, it may grow up to enjoy the average frog's life span of six to eight years.

A tadpole's best defense against its predators is to stay as still as possible and not draw attention to itself. But very few tadpoles survive.

This isn't as bad as it sounds if you remember how many eggs a mother frog lays. Although some of the eggs get gobbled up by enemies, a great many are left to develop into tadpoles. In fact, if only half the tadpoles lived to be adults, we'd be overrun with frogs! As things are, it's estimated that for every 20 eggs laid, one will live long enough to become a frog.

Because tadpoles have tails, and frogs can crawl on the ground, many people think that frogs are reptiles. But neither frogs nor other amphibians are the same as reptiles, which include snakes, turtles, crocodiles, and lizards. A frog has no claws and its skin is smooth. Reptiles have scaly skin, and their feet often have claws. Frogs lay eggs without shells, while reptiles lay eggs that have shells. And a baby frog—a tadpole—doesn't resemble its parents at all. A baby reptile does look like its parents, only a younger version.

The Great Change

As the tadpole grows, it starts to eat more animals than plants. Small water creatures become part of its diet.

Inside the tadpole's body, many incredible changes are taking place. The tadpole's gills gradually change into air-breathing lungs and the tadpole begins to surface for air. Back legs begin to grow: first one, then the other, breaks through the little creature's skin. Next, front legs sprout, the tadpole's mouth widens, and its eyes bulge. Before too long the hind legs are large enough to help with swimming. As each day passes, the tadpole is looking more and more like its parents.

If the developing tadpole loses one of its limbs, all is not lost—a new leg will grow in its place! But this is true only for this stage of its life. When the tadpole becomes an adult frog, it won't be able to replace a leg.

Opposite page: *Though still in its tadpole phase, this little fish-like creature is looking more and more like the Green Frog it will one day be.*

Tadpole or Frog?

When all four legs are fully grown, the tadpole is caught between two worlds. Is it a frog with a tail, or a tadpole with legs? What do you think?

Before it's ready to hop out of the water as an adult frog, a tadpole undergoes one more change. This curious in-between creature stops eating and lives off the food stored in it tail. This "tail food" is slowly absorbed into its body. Once the tail has almost disappeared, there's no doubt about it. The tadpole has become a frog!

For most types of frogs, the whole process from egg to frog takes about two months. But for others, a much longer time is needed. The Bullfrog, for example, takes two whole years to complete it development from tiny egg to full-grown adult frog.

This tadpole still has a tail—but not for long. In fact, frogs are known scientifically as anurans, *which means "without tail."*

A New Beginning

The new frog must now learn how to hop on dry land. The youngster is a little clumsy at first, but soon it's as comfortable on shore as it is in the water. A new chapter in its life has begun.

There are other skills to master, and the new frog learns them quickly. It soon becomes adept at catching food and learns to be alert in order to avoid becoming dinner for a predator. The frog spends the hot summer days immersed in the cool water of a pond. Its big eyes watch all the comings and goings around it.

As autumn approaches, the air and water start turning cooler. Soon winter is on its way. What do frogs do when the weather gets cold?

It's easy to see how the Leopard Frog got its name. From its spots—of course!

The Deep Sleep

Frogs, like all amphibians, are *cold-blooded*—
their bodies can't control their temperature the
way yours does. A frog's temperature rises and
falls with the temperature of the surrounding
air or water. If a frog gets too hot or cold, it
will die. So how does a frog survive winter's
freezing temperatures?

Like many animals, frogs *hibernate,* or go
into a deep sleep for the winter. Some burrow
into the ground, while others simply choose a
sheltered spot under a log or stone. But most
dig themselves into the muddy bottom of a
pond or marsh. There the frogs stop breathing
through their *lungs,* the parts of their bodies
that take in oxygen from the air for use by

the body. Instead, frogs absorb oxygen from the
water through their skin. During hibernation,
a frog's heartbeat slows down greatly, too, and
the frog won't eat or move a muscle until spring.

Eventually warm weather returns, and the
frog climbs out of its winter home to greet the
world with frog song. After the frog mates, the
miraculous cycle of frog life—changing from
egg to tadpole to frog—begins
to unfold all over again.

Frogs and Us

Frogs are not just interesting, they're also useful to people. They help us by eating large numbers of harmful insects. In fact, many gardeners and farmers keep frogs in ponds for this very reason.

But frogs are in trouble. Since about 1995, deformed frogs have been found in many places in the United States and Canada. Some frogs are missing legs and other frogs grow too many of them, while still others grow legs that are misshapen. Scientists are trying to find out why this is happening. Some believe that water and air pollution are contributing to the frog's plight. Other researchers blame *parasites,* creatures that live on or in other creatures. These researchers believe that the tiny parasites bore into tadpoles, causing them to develop in a deformed way. The mystery has not yet been completely solved, but scientists are hard at work trying to discover how we can help our useful and charming—but delicate and troubled—frog neighbors.

Words To Know

Amphibians   One of a group of animals that live both on land and in water. Frogs, toads, newts, and salamanders are amphibians.

Blood vessels   Tubes, arteries, and veins through which blood flows.

Camouflage   Coloring and markings on an animal that blend in with its surroundings.

Cold-blooded   Having a body temperature that stays about the same as the surrounding air or water.

Gills   Openings on a tadpole's head that take in water and remove the oxygen from it.

Habitat   The area or type of area an animal or plant naturally lives in.

Hibernation   A kind of heavy sleep that some animals take in the winter, during which their breathing and heart rates slow, and their body temperature drops.

Lungs   Parts of the body that remove oxygen from the air so that it can be used by the body.

Mate   To come together to produce young.

Oxygen   The part of the air that most living things need to survive.

Parasites   Creatures that live on or in other creatures.

Predator   An animal that lives by hunting other animals.

Prey   An animal hunted by another animal for food.

Sac   A pouch.

Spawn   A mass of frog eggs held together by a jelly-like substance.

Species   A class or kind of animals with certain traits in common.

Sperm   A substance in a male's body that's needed to start new life.

Tadpole   A frog hatchling.

Territory   The area that an animal or group of animals lives in and often defends from other animals of the same kind.

Index

amphibian, 8, 44

bladderwort, 35
blood vessels, 11
body temperature, 44
breathing, 11, 32, 39, 44
Bullfrog, 5, 8, 27, 40

calls, 23, 24, 26, 27, 28
camouflage 23

defense tactics, 23
deformities, 46
diet, 11, 16, 19
distribution, 8

eardrums, 20
eating habits, 11, 16, 32
eggs, 27, 31, 36
enemies, 16, 20, 35, 36
eyelids, 15
eyes, 15, 16, 39, 43

feet, 12, 16, 24, 25
female, 28, 31

gills, 32, 39
habitat, 8, 24
head, 15, 16, 20
hibernation, 44, 45

jelly, 31, 32
jumping, 12

legs, 12, 39, 46
life span, 36

male, 31
mating, 24, 27

polliwog, 35
puffing up, 23

reptiles, 36

senses, 20
singing method, 28
skin, 11, 20
sounds: see calls
spawn, 31, 32
spring, 27
Spring Peeper, 19, 27
summer, 43
swimming, 12, 39

tadpoles, 31, 32, 35, 36, 39, 40
tail, 32, 40
teeth, 16, 32
toads, 5, 8
tongue, 19
tree frogs, 24, 25
types of frogs, 8

vocal sac, 28

winter, 44

PHOTO CREDITS
Cover: Bill Ivy. **Interiors:** Bill Ivy, 4, 6-7, 9, 10, 14, 18, 22, 25, 29, 37, 38, 41, 42. / *Thomas Stack & Associates:* David M. Dennis, 13, 26. / *Ivy Images:* Don Johnston, 17; Robert McCaw, 34. / *Valan Photos:* P. Lewis, 21; Harold V. Green, 30, 33.